Thailand Travel Guide : 60 Things You need to know before traveling to Thailand

Paul Siri

DEDICATION

For my family

CONTENTS

INTRODUCTION

Planning a trip to the exotic Thailand? There's so much to see and experience in the adventurous destination – the food, the breathtaking beaches, the beautiful temples and of course the numerous opportunities to shop and shop till you drop!

Getting into a new place always presents a cultural shock, and doing a little homework in advance will definitely help you make your trip all the more fun and memorable! Here we have jotted down all the possible do's and don'ts to follow when in Thailand and tips and advice to make your vacation enjoyable, comfortable and fun.

When you are heading to Thailand as a tourist, it is easy to get overwhelmed and lose track of where you are headed and what to do. To make sure that you're well prepared for the trip, here is a quick go through of the do's and don'ts to keep in mind. These will not help you interact with people better and find the right places to check out, but also save you from possible issues and problems throughout the visit.

Things to Know Before Traveling to Thailand

The City and the People

The Best Weather – Go during springtime, and avoid going in April because it's way too humid at that time. But on the plus side, the airfare is really cheap and you may enjoy Water festival (Songkran Day).

The people are really courteous – You'll have strangers giving you suggestions on what to do, or just stopping by for the chat. Get ready to be surrounded by super nice people!

There is no concept of queues – You're up for a surprise here. Thais don't stand in lines;

instead there are crowds in public spaces. So make sure to stand your ground!

Dress conservatively – This is especially true when you are visiting a temple, palace or monastery. Women should preferably have their shoulders and legs covered through a long skirt or trousers. Also, cover your elbows and knees to show some respect.

Respect for the King – The King and Royal Family are very highly regarded in Thailand. Don't speak ill, or talk about them it all to avoid any trouble!

Personal hygiene is important – The hot and humid tropical climate of the country requires that you pay extra attention to personal hygiene. Thais are very particular about this and will not hesitate in pointing it out if they notice something off. Take daily showers and wear light, cotton clothing and open toed sandals.

Never throw stuff - This isn't limited to the trash only. Don't throw stuff around on tables or the ground, as it's considered disrespectful and rude.

Respect Thai Courtesy – Thais will never outwardly say no to a request, they will most probably give alternate instructions or even give any answer instead of declining the offer completely.

There will be some natural creatures – Be prepared to see some roaches roaming around and crawling over your feet. Don't freak out!

Score on the deals – You can even find five star hotels for as low as $100 per night. The place ahs some of the best hotel deals to offer!

Choose the right hotels – The most ideal picks for accommodation are places that are near the BTS and MRT stations.

Choose the hostel for your budget – If you want to save the money, you can choose hostel instead of hotel

For more information:

http://www.onceagainhostel.com/#Address

Get massages – Thailand is known for its massage parlors. Check out a few good ones for some relaxation and bliss!

Be prepared for a variety of smells! From flowers to food and sewage, your senses will be bombarded with a ton of different smells throughout the trip.

Don't be fooled by double meanings – A woman too beautiful and flirtatious is probably a lady boy (How to identify the lady boy is in the Bonus topic). Similarly, avoid places that claim to be massage parlors with 'Nice girls' or 'Pretty women'. They are most likely doing more than just massage.

Getting Around

Getting a Cab – Once you head out of the airport, people will come running by at you asking you for a taxi. Beware! They'll overcharge. Go out to the taxi stand instead to hail a cab, which you can sometimes get for 250 Baht.

Language – Basic English is understood in Thailand, and you may also show what you mean and people will be willing to cooperate. You can also learn a few basic phrases in Thai (you can learn in the last chapter) to impress your hosts.

Multiple forms of commute – Thailand has Tuk-Tuks as the most preferred form of commute during the day, while you can hail taxis at night. Also, take advantage of affordable and convenient public transport! Both the BTS (Skytrain) and MRT (Subway) use token systems and maps and are great choices to take you anywhere you want. It is recommended to take a day pass to save cash.

Tuk Tuk

BTS

BTS MAP ROUTE :

http://www.bts.co.th/customer/en/02-route-current_new.aspx

MRT

MRT MAP ROUTE :

http://www.bangkokmetro.co.th/map.as

px?Lang=En&Menu=8

Hail taxis the right way! - Holding your hand with your fingers facing up is considered rude – keep your hands horizontal and the fingers facing down when hailing a cab. Don't clap, snap your fingers or whistle to get their attention.

Don't rely too much on the cab drivers - They may lure you to other places to grab a commission. Don't take their word if they say that a site is closed or shouldn't be visited. Just politely refuse the service, thank them and find another taxi.

Check out the fresh produce –While the street food and fine dining are there, don't forget to check out the fresh produce and fruits. The mangoes of Thailand, incidentally, are the tastiest in the world.

Don't forget the Zoo! Aside from the temples and the beaches, another great place to check out in Thailand is the zoo. Experience one-on-one interaction with exotic wildlife and animals you've never seen before!

Food and Drink

Use your spoon – People in Thailand use spoons to eat and not the fork.

Check out the 7-11s – There are probably more 7-11s in Thailand than Starbucks in America!

Don't go for Meal Inclusive Hotel Packages – Savor the local delicacies and street food instead, that will be cheaper and much more fun! Go for complimentary breakfast at hotel if you want.

Communicate with Waiters – When beckoning a waiter, keep your palm down and move your fingers up and down. Holding your hand or fingers up is not recommended.

Be wary of the Street Food – Bangkok Belly is a real thing, so unless you want to spend your holiday throwing up, avoid eating from unhygienic stalls or places where cats are roaming around.

Be careful what you ask for – Water or beer? Popular beer brands like Chang or Singha offer both beer and water. Tell your attendant clearly which one do you want to save any surprises!

Singha **BEER**

Singha **WATER**

Now it's time to Shop!

Shopping in Thailand

What's a holiday without the shopping? Thailand offers amazing deals and great bargains on local artefacts, clothes, bags, shoes, jewellery and more – provided you know how to negotiate the prices. Here are a few tips on doing that:

Find places with a lot of street shops. With so much competition, you'll be able to score a great deal!

Recommended : Khaosan Road, China Town(Yaowarat Road), JJ market(Jatujak market)

Khasan Road

China Town

JJ Market

Smile around, be nice, and courteous. You'll be surprised how much this will help you out.

Make your calculations – Even if you think something looks like a great bargain, do the mental math and calculate the amount you are spending in dollars. Then decide whether you are ready to pay that much for that item.

Be prepared to walk away – If you think something is too expensive, show your dismay and walk away. They'll most probably call you back. However, show that you are interested in their merchandise and not just wasting their time.

Play it out – Put some extra money, say 100 baht, in one pocket and nothing else. If they aren't willing to negotiate on the price tell them this is all you have and if they don't agree still, politely excuse and leave. They'll rarely let someone walk away once they have seen the money.

Don't bargain or haggle with taxi drivers. Make them drive you by the meter instead.

Always test what you are buying. Especially if you are buying electronic items, CDs, DVDs or headsets.

Shopkeepers will probably raise the prices for foreigners. If you have a Thai friend with you, ask them to handle the money matters!

> **Tip 1**: If you like an item a lot, don't ask the shopkeeper straightaway for its price as they are likely to raise it high. Instead ask for something else's price and casually inquire about the rate for the item that you want as an afterthought.

> **Tip** 2: Have change at the ready. If you have bargained or haggled on a price and brought it down, pay them the exact amount in change. They may say

that they have no change just to get the note.

Avoiding Tourist Traps

Being smart on your feet is important, as there are always people who will try and take advantage of you as an unsuspecting tourist.

Here is some advice and guidance on steering clear of trouble:

1. Don't listen to touts at the airport or malls, as they are most likely to overcharge you for everything or suggest places that get them a commission.

2. Instead of bargaining with a taxi driver, always go for a cab that has a meter (lights on top of the taxi). You can also

decide on a rate if you think it's feasible enough for the distance.

3. If you need advice on where to shop, the best place to ask and get good leads is your hotel.

4. Dress respectfully when going in a temple, which means no sleeveless shirts or shorts. Avoid talking too loudly, leave your shoes outside and don't point at or touch the head or feet of a monk or even the statue of Buddha.

5. Always consult the Jewel Fest Club or the Thai Gem and Jewelry Traders Association before buying precious stones

and gems in Thailand. If a deal sounds too good to be true, it probably isn't.

6. When going to Patpong or any other red light district area, avoid dark alleys, upper floors or places that don't have a lot of people as they may corner foreigners there and demand to pay a hefty bill.

7. People like bar girls may try to trick you by telling you a sad story of a sibling needing surgery or no funds for education or living. Be careful of them as they are usually after your money. Politely refuse the offer but don't disrespect them.

Visiting Temples in Thailand

Being inside a Buddhist monastery and learning about the culture, traditions and beliefs of Buddhists in Thailand can be an enriching experience. However, there is a certain level of respect and etiquette to be followed at these spots, and knowing about it in advance can save you from embarrassment in the future. Here you go:

1. **The clothing** – The most important thing to be careful about is your attire. Wear covered, long dresses with a modest neckline and everything above the elbows and ankles covered. Long skirts and trousers are recommended with sandals, though the shoes have to be left out of the temple. Dressing in all black isn't recommended.

2. **Avoid jewellery** – Show of wealth is considered disrespectful so avoid flashy jewellery and ornaments.

3. **Greeting with a 'Wai'** – Greet monks by bowing your head down, pressing your palms together and taking them to your forehead. This is a greeting of respect and

is called a Wai.

4. **Take care with photographs** - Don't climb on, touch or even pose with statues of Buddha. Not even if they are broken or damaged.

5. **Shoes can't be taken inside a temple,** as it's considered very rude.

6. Women are not advised to be alone with, flirt with or speak suggestively to monks.

7. Don't touch the feet or the head of a Buddha statue.

8. Don't walk in front of people bowing.

9. Alcohol shouldn't be taken inside a temple or monastery.

10. Do not kill any insect.

11. Don't step over the threshold.

12. Shuffle on your knees if you have to walk past a seated monk.

13. For food offerings, don't touch the alms bowl's edges with a spoon. Also, pour water in the libation jar suing both hands.

Speaking in Thai

Although basic English will work at most spots in Thailand, it's always good to know a few phrases in Thai that will help you communicate better with people.

It's common courtesy to end sentences with **ka** if you are a girl or a woman and **krap** if you are a boy or a man. For example, saying "Thank you" a girl or a woman would be say "Khob khun **ka**" and a boy or a man would be say "Khob khun **krap**".

Here are some common phrases that you can learn:

- Sa wad dee ka means Hello
- Phom cheu _____ means My name is _____ (for men)
- Chan cheu_____ means My name is _____ (for women)
- Khob khun means Thank you.
- Mai ow means No, thank you.
- Sabai dee mai means How are you?
- Sabai dee means I'm fine.
- Khor toat means Sorry.
- Tao rie means How much?
- Lot noy dai mai means Can you lower the price?
- Khoy pap nueng means Wait.
- Phee krab/ka means Excuse me waiter (male/female)
- Khun poot Angrit dai mai means Do you speak English?

Although basic English will work at most spots in Thailand, it's always good to know a few

Bonus Tips: Identifying a Lady Boy in Thailand

A lady boy is a male-to-female transgender person and is quite common in Thailand. They are beautiful and mostly work in the entertainment industry. Recognizing them straightaway is difficult, but there are always clues that you can look out for, which include:

- They may have certain manly biological signs like Adam's apple, the male genitalia, large hand and feet, tall height, angular features, wide shoulders as compared to hips etc.

- Their voices are deeper and they will most often speak softly to hide it.

- Their style of walking is mostly flirty, as is their attitude towards men.

- Their wrists are usually straight, as opposed to females who have dainty fingers and slightly slanted hands.

About The Author

He is a travel junkie! Writing about anything that involves tourism, new places and fun, adventurous destinations excites him like nothing else. Also, He have experience writing guides, travelogues, how-to's and DIYs, which makes him proud and excited writing this book

Thank you

Thank you again for downloading this book!

I hope you enjoyed reading about my book on all the information on thing to know before go to Thailand, shopping in Thailand, avoiding tourist traps visiting temple in Thailand and bonus tip to identify Lady boy in Thailand. we have compiled all the information in easy to read format!

Finally, if you enjoyed this book, please take the time to share your thoughts and **post a review on Amazon**. It'd be greatly appreciated!

Thank you!

DID YOU KNOW?

* Authors are not rich. In fact, most make less than $10, 000 a year. Being an author is a SMALL BUSINESS

* If there are 50 reviews, Amazon lists a book in its newsletters and other promotions (Also Boughts)

* REVIEWS are the easiest way to say THANK YOU to an author and tell their publisher to produce more books.

* Reviews can be short: "I LIKED IT". It's the number of reviews that matters the most.

SUPPORT AUTHORS
SUPPORT SMALL
BUSINESS

www.tallpoppies.org

Made in the USA
Las Vegas, NV
16 December 2023